Confessions of a Godly Mother

Prayers of the Heart

Cassandra V. Fulwood

Copyright © 2025 by Cassandra V. Fulwood

All rights reserved. This book or parts thereof may not be reproduced, stored in a retrieval system, or transmitted in any form or by any means–electronic, mechanical, photocopy, recording, scanning, or otherwise–except for brief quotations in critical reviews or articles, without the prior written permission of the publisher.

Published in West Palm Beach, Florida, by Cassy's Touch Publishing, LLC. www.cassystouch.com

The publisher is not responsible for websites (or their content) not owned by the publisher.

Scripture quotations marked KJV are taken from the King James Version. Public domain.

Scriptures taken from the Holy Bible, New International Version®, NIV®. Copyright © 1973, 1978, 1984, 2011 by Biblica, Inc.™ Used by permission of Zondervan. All rights reserved worldwide. www.zondervan.com The "NIV" and "New International Version" are trademarks registered in the United States Patent and Trademark Office by Biblica, Inc.™

Scripture taken from the New King James Version®. Copyright © 1982 by Thomas Nelson. Used by permission. All rights reserved.

Visit the author's website at CassandraFulwood.com.

ISBN: 979-8-9892358-4-1 (hardcover)

Library of Congress Control Number 2025906482

Printed in the United States of America

This Book is Dedicated...

To my Godly mother, Lillie.

To every godly woman who has ever
stood in the gap for a child, whether your own,
a grandchild, a godchild, a student, a neighbor's child,
the child of a friend or coworker...This is for you.

To the women who have labored in prayer,
wept in silence, and refused to give up, regardless of
the child's age, choices, or season of life...

To those who have never birthed a child yet have
mothered through intercession, mentorship, and
unwavering love...

To the mother who's asked through tears,
"Where did I go wrong?"—you are not alone.
Your heartbreak is seen. Your faith is honored.
Your prayers are still working.

You're in good company here.
Thank you for choosing to walk this journey with me.

This book is for you.

Table of Contents

Introduction	1
How to Use *Confessions of A Godly Mother*	5
Scriptural Foundation for This Book	7
Something to Think About	8

Part 1: Holding Hearts Through The Years

1. When They're in the Womb — 11
2. When They're Babies & Toddlers — 16
3. When They're School-Aged — 21
4. When They're Teenagers — 26
5. When They're Young Adults — 31
6. When They're Grown — 36

Part 2: Sacred Warfare: A Mother's Call to Battle

7. When They're Prodigal — 43
8. When You've Experienced Loss — 48
9. When You're Parenting with Pain — 53
10. When You're Co-Parenting or Single — 58
11. When You're A Spiritual Mother — 63
12. When They're Struggling with Mental Health — 68

13. When You're Battling Shame As A Mother	73
14. When You're Praying for Generations To Come	78
15. When You Feel Spiritually Empty	83
16. When They're Called Into Ministry	88
17. When You're Praying Through A Crisis	93

Part 3: The PowerSpeak Toolkit

Declarations About Your Children	99
Blessings to Confess Over Your Children	105
Prayers for the Mother's Soul	107
Scriptures to Meditate Upon Regarding Your Children	111
Afterword	115

Introduction

Confessions of a Godly Mother was born not from a place of perfection but from the sacred tension of motherhood where joy and exhaustion meet, where faith is tested often, where motherhood and intercession collide, where the cries of a mother reach the ears of Heaven, where whispered prayers spoken in the quiet of midnight carry the authority to break generational cycles, and where a mother's prayers can shift the legacy of generations.

Motherhood is one of the highest callings a woman can walk in, not because it is always visible or celebrated, but because it is deeply spiritual. It is a ministry of formation. It is the ministry of shaping lives, stewarding destinies, and contending for souls.

Motherhood is layered with joy, fear, hope, heartbreak, growth, and surrender. Some days, you will feel strong and Spirit-filled. Other days, you may feel broken and barely holding on. This book meets you in both places.

Cassandra V. Fulwood

The world may tell you that your influence is limited to the walls of your home, but the truth is that your prayers stretch far beyond those walls. Your whispered scriptures in the night, your tears soaked into pillowcases, and your declarations over sleeping children are acts of war in the Spirit.

This book is for every mother who has ever questioned if she was doing enough. It's for the mother who's parenting through pain. For the one who feels invisible behind laundry piles and lunch boxes. For the mother who prays through tears. For the mother who feels unseen while raising children who are still learning to see. For the mother of a prodigal who hasn't lost faith.

For the mother battling guilt from yesterday, fear for today, and questions about tomorrow. For the single mom, the stepmom, the spiritual mom, the grieving mom, the praying grandmother, and the supportive godmother. This book is for every woman who has felt the weight of motherhood and still chose to kneel. It's for the ones who carry both hope and heartbreak, who've laid awake wondering, *"Lord, are You really listening? When will You come through?"* For the mothers tired of apologizing to God for not getting it all right, this book will remind you that God never asked for perfection. He asked for your presence.

No judgment, just grace. No pressure, just permission to bring your whole self to the feet of Jesus. Come as the woman you are—imperfect, poured out, and still full of love. Come ready to confess God's promises and watch them bear fruit. Come ready to walk in the fullness of your identity as a godly mother.

Within these pages, you'll find raw honesty, prophetic declarations, and daily confessions grounded in Scripture and seasoned with grace. Each chapter meets you in a different season of motherhood: when your child is in the womb, when they're grown, walking with God, or running far from Him. You'll walk through devotions for your weary days, blessings to confess over your children, and journal prompts to keep you grounded in truth.

This book is a tool to remind you that you are not just a mom—you are a watchman on the wall, a gatekeeper, a spiritual authority in your home, and a daughter of the King entrusted with the lives of future Kingdom Builders.

We are living in a time where culture is loud, identity is attacked, and families are under pressure like never before. The enemy is targeting the next generation, but he is also targeting the mothers who are called to guard them. But a mother who prays is a mother who pushes back darkness. When a godly mother confesses truth over her children, over her house, over her own weary heart, something shifts.

This book is your spiritual arsenal. It is your morning whisper and evening warfare. Your reminder that God has not forgotten you and that your prayers are not hitting the ceiling. They're building legacy. It is more than a book. It's a healing balm for the soul of every mother who still believes in the power of her prayers.

I hope that as you read, you'll not only find language for your journey but that your confessions will become declarations, and your declarations will shape destinies because your prayers matter. Your words carry weight. Your role as a godly mother is not only essential—it's eternal.

Welcome to the front lines.
Welcome to legacy building.
Welcome to *Confessions of a Godly Mother*.

With faith, favor, focus, fervent prayer, & fierce love,
Cassandra V. Fulwood

How to Use *Confessions of a Godly Mother*

This book was designed to walk with you. Use it at your own pace, in your own rhythm, and with the freedom to come back to chapters as needed. Whether you're in a peaceful season or a spiritual battle, this book is here to equip, encourage, and strengthen you.

Here are a few simple ways to get the most out of your journey:

- Read one chapter per day or week – Let the themes speak to your season. Pause, reflect, and allow Holy Spirit to highlight what you need most.

- Speak the confessions and declarations aloud – There is power in your voice. Proclaim truth even if you don't feel it yet. Your words are planting seeds.

- Write in the journal sections – Let your heart respond to the prompts. Invite God into your motherhood story as you reflect, release, and renew.

- Use The PowerSpeak Toolkit as a regular prayer guide – Whether it's morning blessings, topic-based declarations, or a devotional moment during nap time, let these tools become part of your daily rhythm.

- Come back often – Different chapters will speak louder in different seasons. Highlight what stands out, revisit what heals, and celebrate what God restores.

- Invite others in – Consider using this book in a small group, mom circle, or prayer partner setting. There is strength when mothers pray together.

Scriptural Foundation for This Book

- Proverbs 31:28 (KJV) – *"Her children arise up, and call her blessed; her husband also, and he praiseth her."*

- Isaiah 54:13 (NKJV) – *"All your children shall be taught by the Lord, and great shall be the peace of your children."*

- Psalm 127:3 (NKJV) – *"Behold, children are a heritage from the Lord, the fruit of the womb is a reward."*

- 2 Timothy 1:5 (NKJV) – *"When I call to remembrance the genuine faith that is in you, which dwelt first in your grandmother Lois and your mother Eunice, and I am persuaded is in you also."*

- Lamentations 2:19 (NKJV) – *"Arise, cry out in the night, at the beginning of the watches; pour out your heart like water before the face of the Lord. Lift your hands toward Him for the life of your young children…"*

Something to Think About

Confessions vs. Declarations

The difference between confession of the Scriptures and declarations of the Scriptures lies in their intent, focus, and application.

Confession of the Scriptures:

- Comes from the Greek word *homologeo* (ὁμολογέω), meaning "to say the same thing as," "to agree with," or "to acknowledge."
- Involves agreeing with and affirming God's Word as truth.
- Often used for personal transformation, faith-building, and repentance.
- Example: If you are struggling with fear, you might confess 2 Timothy 1:7: *"God has not given me a spirit of fear, but of power, love, and a sound mind."*

    You are aligning yourself with what God has already spoken.

Declarations of the Scriptures:

- A bold, authoritative proclamation of God's truth.
- Often used for spiritual warfare, speaking into situations, and shifting atmospheres.
- Example: Instead of merely confessing 2 Timothy 1:7, you would declare: *"I walk in power, love, and a sound mind! Fear has no place in my life. I am victorious in Christ!"*

    This is speaking God's will with divine authority.

Conclusion:

- Confession aligns your heart and mind with God's truth.
- Declarations speak that truth with authority into the spiritual and natural realm.
- Both are biblical and powerful.

Cassandra V. Fulwood

Part 1:
Holding Hearts Through The Years

Chapter 1

When They're in the Womb

Praying Life, Purpose, and Protection

*"Before I formed you in the womb I knew you;
before you were born
I sanctified you..." – Jeremiah 1:5 (NKJV)*

Reflection

Motherhood begins before you hear the first cry. It begins in the quiet space where life is growing and forming. Sometimes long before a positive pregnancy test. Sometimes after years of waiting. Sometimes unexpectedly.

As a godly mother, you are already in a position to speak life into the unseen. Your words of faith are more powerful than a sonogram. Whether your pregnancy is joyful or complicated. Whether you've experienced loss or are filled with anticipation, this sacred season calls you to declare heaven's identity over the life within you.

You are not just carrying a child. You are carrying a purpose, a calling, a destiny wrapped in skin. You are already their first intercessor. Every whisper of scripture, every tear of surrender, every song over your womb, it matters.

Biblical Example: *Hannah* (1 Samuel 1:10-20)

Hannah wept bitterly and prayed fervently for a child. Her desperation was not weakness; it was the beginning of her calling as a godly mother. She vowed to give her son back to the Lord, and when Samuel was born, she kept her promise. Samuel would go on to become one of Israel's greatest prophets. It is certain that Hannah's fervent prayers gave entryway to this—before he was even born.

Confessions & Declarations
Speak these aloud daily over yourself and your unborn child:

> "I am a godly mother, chosen to carry life and purpose."

> "My womb is blessed and protected. God is forming greatness inside me."

"I speak peace, strength, and divine alignment into my body and my baby's development."

"This child belongs to God, and I entrust their future to Him."

"I declare that this child will fulfill their God-given destiny."

"No weapon formed against me or my baby will prosper."

"My child is growing in wisdom, favor, and divine strength even now."

"The Lord is knitting together every part of their body and purpose according to His perfect plan."

Prayer

Heavenly Father, I thank You for the miracle of life growing inside me. I surrender this child to You, just as Hannah did. Form them not just physically but spiritually. Anoint them even now for Your work. Keep me in perfect peace as I trust in You. I silence every fear and release Your Word over this pregnancy. This child is fearfully and wonderfully made. In the creative name of Jesus Christ, Amen.

Journal Prompt

What fears or expectations do I need to release to God during this pregnancy?

What has God shown me or spoken to me about the life I carry?

Confessions of A Godly Mother

Chapter 2

When They're Babies & Toddlers

Praying Peace, Safety, and Spiritual Foundation

*"You will keep him in perfect peace,
whose mind is stayed on You,
because he trusts in You." – Isaiah 26:3 (NKJV)*

Reflection

The baby stage is beautiful, exhausting, and often overwhelming. Sleepless nights, unpredictable cries, growth milestones, and new routines can make even the most devoted mother feel unsure and weary. But Godly motherhood in this stage is not about perfection. It's about presence, peace, and prayer.

You're not just meeting physical needs. You're shaping emotional security and spiritual awareness. When you hold your child, you're covering them in more than warmth. You're covering them in prayer. Your whispers, lullabies, and worship songs teach their spirit to rest in God. And your prayers? They're doing more than calming them in the moment. They're planting seeds for a lifetime.

You may not see the fruit yet. But every peaceful nap, song of worship, and verse spoken aloud is forming a strong foundation. Peace is not the absence of crying. It's the presence of God in your mothering.

Biblical Example: *Mary and Jesus* (Luke 2:19)

After the shepherds visited baby Jesus, the Bible says Mary *"treasured up all these things and pondered them in her heart."* Though young and likely unsure, Mary was present, attentive, and spiritually aware. She didn't fully understand who her child would become but covered Him in quiet faith and holy responsibility.

You, too, are raising greatness, even when it's wrapped in diapers.

Confessions & Declarations
Speak these truths aloud over yourself and your baby and toddler:

"I am equipped by God to nurture this child in love and patience."

"God is giving me grace for sleepless nights and long days."

"My child is safe, secure, and surrounded by God's presence."

"Even in chaos, God is with me, and peace is in this home."

"I declare that my baby is growing strong in body, mind, and spirit."

"Peace will reign in our home, and joy will fill our days."

"Every word I speak over my child will shape them in faith, security, and love."

"The Spirit of God rests on this child, and their heart is tender to His voice from infancy."

Prayer

Lord, thank You for the gift of my child. Even in my exhaustion, I praise You for the opportunity to mother with grace. Cover this child in Your peace and protection. Let my home be a place where Your presence dwells. May my voice carry life, and my hands carry love. I surrender this season to You. Give me the patience, joy, and discernment I need. In Jesus' name, Amen.

Journal Prompt

What are the biggest challenges I face in this season of parenting?

How can I invite God's peace and presence into my home in a tangible way?

Cassandra V. Fulwood

Chapter 3

When They're School-Aged

Praying Wisdom, Confidence, and Godly Character

*"A wise man will hear and increase learning,
and a man of understanding will attain wise counsel."*
– Proverbs 1:5 (NKJV)

Reflection

As your child begins school, they are stepping out into a world filled with voices, such as teachers, peers, media, and experiences that will start shaping their thinking and self-worth. This season can bring a mix of pride and panic as they grow more independent, ask more questions, and face both opportunities and obstacles.

But Mama, don't fear what's outside. Strengthen what's inside.

This is a time for you to pray bold, intentional prayers over your child's mind, heart, friendships, and sense of identity. Your prayers go ahead of them to the lunchroom, the playground, the classroom, and every social setting. You may not be physically present, but your intercession anchors them in the Spirit.

This is the season where you begin equipping them not just with school supplies but with scriptural truth, godly character, and spiritual covering. Your confessions teach them who they are, and Whose they are.

Biblical Example: *Moses' Mother* – *Jochebed* (Exodus 2:1-10)

Jochebed had to release her child into the world...literally into the river, and she did so with faith. She built a basket and trusted God to guide, protect, and preserve Moses' life. Even when we release our children into school, activities, and influences beyond our control, we can do so knowing that God is still in control. Like Moses, our children can be raised in a secular system and still carry divine destiny because they are covered in prayer.

Confessions & Declarations

Speak these aloud over your school-aged child every day:

"My child is learning with joy, wisdom, and clarity."

"They are surrounded by good friends and godly influences."

"No word spoken over them will shape them more than God's Word."

"They are secure in their identity and rooted in truth."

"I declare that my child will be a leader and not a follower."

"They are protected from bullying, deception, and confusion."

"They will excel in every subject and grow in wisdom and stature."

"They will love learning, respect authority, and reflect the character of Christ."

Prayer

Heavenly Father, thank You for this season of growth. As my child learns and explores the world around them, help them to be anchored in Your truth. Give them wisdom, courage, and understanding. Place the right friends and mentors in their lives. I surrender my anxiety and choose to trust Your covering. Go with them to school, surround them with peace, and guide their every step. In Jesus' name, Amen.

Journal Prompt

What do I need to trust God with concerning my child's school life?

What specific qualities or godly character traits do I want to see grow in my child this season?

Confessions of A Godly Mother

Chapter 4

When They're Teenagers

Praying Identity, Purity, and
Purpose During Seasons of Change

"Let no one despise your youth, but be an example to the believers in word, in conduct, in love, in spirit, in faith, in purity." – 1 Timothy 4:12 (NKJV)

Reflection

The teen years are like a bridge: one foot in childhood and the other stepping toward adulthood. This season is marked by transition, questions, testing boundaries, and forming identity. Hormones are high. Emotions run deep. As a mother, your role shifts again. You are no longer just a protector. You are a guide, a counselor, and more than ever, an intercessor.

Don't be discouraged by their growing independence. That's by God's design. Your job isn't to control them. It's to cover them. You do that best through prayer and Spirit-led conversations. Their ears may not always listen, but their spirit hears what your prayers declare.

Your teenager needs clarity in a world of confusion, purity in a culture of compromise, and truth in a time of lies. That's why your confessions must go before them daily to strengthen their discernment and call forth the destiny God placed inside them before birth.

Biblical Example: *Jesus as a Teen (Luke 2:41–52)*

At just twelve years old, Jesus was found in the temple engaging in deep conversations with religious leaders. When Mary and Joseph found Him, Jesus responded with purpose: *"Did you not know that I must be about My Father's business?"* Though He returned with them in obedience, this glimpse into His teenage years shows us that purpose begins early. A praying mother, like Mary, may not always understand her teen, but she can treasure every word, moment, and promise in her heart. She can and must continue praying.

Confessions & Declarations
Speak these aloud daily over your teenager…even if

they roll their eyes:

> "My teenager is not lost. They are loved and led by God."
>
> "I trust God to complete the work He has started in them."
>
> "Even in their confusion or rebellion, God is pursuing them with relentless love."
>
> "My child will not be swallowed by culture. They are covered by Christ."
>
> "I declare that my teenager walks in purity, wisdom, and purpose."
>
> "They will not be influenced by darkness but will shine as a bright light in their generation."
>
> "Their mind is sharp, their spirit is discerning, and their heart is open to truth."
>
> "They will hear God's voice above every other voice and make decisions that lead to life."

Prayer

Father, this season of parenting feels different and harder than ever. My teenager is growing, changing, and facing things I never imagined. But You see them, know them, and love them more than I do. Surround them with godly friends, mentors, and influences. Keep them from harm, temptation, and deception. Teach me how to love without being overbearing and to pray with fierce faith. In Jesus' name, Amen.

Journal Prompt

What are the biggest fears or concerns I have about my teenager right now?

How can I shift from worrying about them to warring in prayer for them?

Cassandra V. Fulwood

Chapter 5

When They're Young Adults

Praying Direction, Discernment,
and Destiny Over Their Independence

"The steps of a good man are ordered by the Lord, and He delights in his way." – Psalm 37:23 (NKJV)

Reflection

They're out of the house. Maybe they're in college, in their first apartment, working a job, navigating relationships, or wandering through life trying to find themselves. Whatever the case, You're no longer steering the wheel. You're watching from the passenger seat.

But don't confuse distance with disconnection. Your prayers still carry authority, legacy, and weight. Your words still matter. Your faith still builds a hedge of protection and direction even if they don't text back.

In this season, you're not raising them anymore; you're releasing them. Do so with confidence that God is the same yesterday, today, and forever. He's just as much with them now as when they took their first steps.

This stage isn't about managing. It's about modeling and mentoring in the Spirit. About releasing control but never releasing your posture in prayer. Your declarations over them matter more now than ever.

Biblical Example: *The Mother of James and John* (Matthew 20:20–23)

This mother boldly approached Jesus and asked, *"Grant that these two sons of mine may sit, one on Your right hand and the other on the left, in Your kingdom."* She wasn't just concerned about their physical life. She was invested in their eternal destiny. Though Jesus redirected her request, her heart posture teaches us that a godly mother never stops interceding for her children's position and purpose in the Kingdom.

Confessions & Declarations
Speak these over your young adult children consistently, whether they're near or far:

"My child is not out of reach. They are in God's hands."

"I release them from my control and entrust them fully to God's divine plan."

"They may be grown, but they are still growing. God is faithful to finish the work He began."

"I speak peace over their mind, direction over their decisions, and protection over their path."

"I declare that my young adult child walks in godly wisdom and makes sound decisions."

"They are sensitive to Holy Spirit and led by truth, not trends."

"They will walk in integrity, pursue purpose, and fulfill their Kingdom assignment."

"They are surrounded by the right people, aligned with the right opportunities, and walking the right path."

Prayer

Lord, You know where my child is physically, emotionally, and spiritually. I surrender my desire to control and choose instead to cover them in faith. Go where I cannot go. Speak where I cannot speak. Protect them from harmful decisions, strengthen them in moments of weakness, and remind them constantly that they are never alone. May Your Word be a lamp for their feet and a light on their path. I bless their journey, and I trust You to lead them into all truth. In Jesus' name, Amen.

Journal Prompt

What do I need to release in this season concerning my child?

Where do I see God at work in their life, even if it's small?

Confessions of A Godly Mother

Chapter 6

When They're Grown

Praying Legacy, Wisdom, and Lifelong Faithfulness

"Being confident of this very thing, that He who has begun a good work in you will complete it until the day of Jesus Christ." – Philippians 1:6 (NKJV)

Reflection

They're grown now. Making their own decisions. Raising families of their own. Building careers, navigating adulthood, or perhaps still searching for their way. Some are close; some may be distant. One thing hasn't changed, and that is the fact that you are still their mother, and your voice in the Spirit still matters.

The world may tell you your influence is over. Heaven disagrees. You may no longer make their schedules or pack their lunches, but you can still pack their lives with prayer.

Godly motherhood doesn't retire. It matures. In this season, your role is legacy-building, speaking blessings, wisdom, and destiny into your children and your children's children. You pray not just for their journey, but for the generations that will come through them.

Whether your adult child is strong in faith or wandering far, your words remain a prophetic covering. You are still sowing into the soil of their souls through prayer and intercession.

Biblical Example: *Samson's Mother* (Judges 13–16)

Samson's mother was entrusted with the divine assignment to carry and raise a child marked by God for a unique purpose. She received her instructions directly from an angel. She obeyed with reverence, understanding Samson's consecration even before he was born. But once he was grown, she had to release him.

Like so many godly mothers, she watched from a distance as her son, who was called, anointed, and set apart, made reckless decisions, aligned with the wrong people, and stepped outside the boundaries of his divine identity. Yet, Scripture never tells us that she stopped believing, and neither should you.

She had done her part. She had planted the seed. In the end, when the dust settled, even in his blindness and brokenness, Samson remembered his God, fulfilled his purpose, and was counted among the faithful (Hebrews 11:32).

Even when your grown child drifts, God has not forgotten the calling on their life. Even when you can no longer guide with your hands, your prayers can still cover them like a mantle.

You may not be able to control their choices, but you can stand firm in faith, trusting the God who began the work to bring it to completion.

Confessions & Declarations
Pray and declare these over your grown child—no matter their season of life:

> "My child is never too old for my prayers and never too far for God's reach."

> "God is still writing their story, and I trust Him with every chapter."

> "I honor the adult they are becoming, and I cover them with grace and truth."

"My legacy as a mother lives on through actions and faith-filled words."

"I declare that my grown child walks in wisdom and seeks the Lord in all they do."

"They are blessed in their relationships, work, and decisions."

"They are aligned with Kingdom purpose and set apart for God's glory."

"They will leave a legacy of faith, honor, and integrity for the next generation."

Prayer

Father, thank You for the journey of motherhood and for walking with me through every stage. My children are grown now, but my love and prayers for them remain strong. Bless the work of their hands. Heal the places in them I cannot reach. Encourage them when life feels heavy. Remind them who they are and Whose they are. Use me to speak blessing and wisdom. When they are reluctant to listen, send other Christ-followers across their paths to speak Your life into them. Let my life be a testimony of unwavering faith. In Jesus' name, Amen.

Journal Prompt

What has God taught me through parenting adult children?

How can I continue to support them spiritually without overstepping?

Confessions of A Godly Mother

Cassandra V. Fulwood

Part 2:

Sacred Warfare:
A Mother's Call to Battle

Chapter 7

When They're Prodigal

Praying Return, Repentance, and Restoration Over a Wandering Child

"Train up a child in the way he should go, and when he is old he will not depart from it." – Proverbs 22:6 (NKJV)

Reflection

There's a unique ache in the heart of a mother who watches her child walk away from the truth she prayed into them. Whether it's a slow drifting or a bold rebellion, the pain feels like a tear in your soul. You replay their childhood, question your choices, and wonder where it all turned.

But Mama, let this truth anchor your soul: what was planted in love and truth is not dead. It's just dormant. Your child may be far from God right now, but Holy Spirit knows their location, their language, and the softest place in their heart.

This is not the time to give up. This is the time to war in the Spirit. Your tears are intercession. Your declarations are life. Your prayers are pulling them back from the edge, even when you can't see it yet.

Biblical Example: *The Prodigal Son (Luke 15:11–24)*

Jesus told the story of a son who took his inheritance, wandered far, and lost everything. But the father didn't chase him. He watched. He waited. When his son returned, it was obvious the father was waiting with expectation. He ran to meet him with compassion and full restoration.

God's heart for your child is even greater than your own. He's not done writing their story.

Confessions & Declarations
Speak these truths out loud, whether they're in your home or far away:

> "My child belongs to God, and He is calling them back."

"The truth they once knew is still alive in their heart."

"I will not parent in fear. I will stand in faith."

"My prayers are planting seeds, tearing down strongholds, and preparing the way home."

"I declare that my prodigal child is returning to the Lord!"

"Every lie is being replaced with truth, and every chain is being broken."

"The Spirit of God is chasing them down with love, mercy, and conviction."

"They will come home spiritually, emotionally, and relationally, and their testimony will be powerful."

Prayer

Father, I lift my child before You. You know where they are physically and spiritually. I speak Your truth over every lie they've believed. Soften their heart. Interrupt their plans. Surround them with divine encounters and relentless grace. I release them from my grip and place them fully in Your hands. Bring them home. Not just to me, but to You. In Jesus' name, Amen.

Journal Prompt

How can I shift from pleading in fear to praying in faith for my prodigal child?

What scriptures or promises am I standing on for their return?

Confessions of A Godly Mother

Chapter 8

When You've Experienced Loss

Praying Through Grief, Healing, and
Hope After Losing a Child or the Hope of One

*"The Lord is near to those who have a broken heart,
and saves such as have a contrite spirit."*
– Psalm 34:18 (NKJV)

Reflection

This chapter is sacred. It's for the mother whose arms feel empty, whose prayers feel unanswered, and whose heart is quietly shattered. Whether your loss came through miscarriage, stillbirth, infertility, or the tragic death of a child you once held in your arms, you are still a mother.

Loss doesn't erase the title. It doesn't silence the bond. It doesn't disqualify the seeds of prayer you've sown.

Grief is holy ground. As a godly mother, you are invited to weep in God's presence, not apart from it. He sees every tear. He counts every ache. And in ways we may never understand, He redeems even this.

You may feel like your prayers failed. They did not. Every one of them reached heaven. Though your child may not be with you, they are held by the very One who heard your prayers.

Biblical Example: *Rizpah and her sons* (2 Samuel 21:1–10)

Rizpah was the mother of two sons who were executed as part of a political atonement for Saul's sins. Her sons were handed over to death, and their bodies were exposed on a hillside and left unburied, dishonored, and vulnerable. But Rizpah stayed with them. Her action still echoes through eternity.

She laid out sackcloth on a rock and kept vigil over their remains for months from the beginning of the harvest until the rains fell from heaven. She beat away the vultures by day and the wild animals by night. Her actions were not just a cry of grief. They were an act of sacred warfare.

Rizpah teaches us that a mother's love has prophetic power even in profound loss. Her steadfastness moved the heart of King David, who honored her sons with a proper burial; thereby, restoring dignity and bringing her much needed closure.

Loss may change your role as a mother, but it does not cancel your voice. You may be grieving, but you still have spiritual authority. You may not have answers, but you will endure. God sees, and He honors your tears. He understands and remembers your pain.

Confessions & Declarations
Speak these even through tears because your healing begins with truth:

"I am still a mother even if my arms feel empty."

"God is healing my heart, and I am safe to grieve in His presence."

"This loss does not mean God abandoned me. He is with me in every wave of sorrow."

"My child's life, no matter how brief, was meaningful, loved, and known by God."

"I declare that healing is rising in my heart, even as I grieve."

"Joy will come again, and hope will not disappoint me."

"God is restoring the pieces of my heart with His perfect love."

"My story will speak of strength, grace, and the faithfulness of God even in loss."

Prayer

Father, You know the pain I carry. You know the child I longed for or the one I held and lost. Thank You for being the God who sees and stays. Wrap me in Your comfort. Speak peace to my grief and remind me daily that this child was not forgotten or forsaken. Let healing begin. Not by forgetting but by remembering with hope. Thank You for holding what I can't. In Jesus' name, Amen.

Journal Prompt

What do I need to surrender to God about this loss?

How has God met me in my pain and how do I want Him to meet me still?

Cassandra V. Fulwood

Chapter 9

When You're Parenting with Pain

Praying Through Exhaustion, Heartbreak, and Hidden Battles

"Come to Me, all you who labor and are heavy laden, and I will give you rest." – Matthew 11:28 (NKJV)

Reflection

Motherhood doesn't pause when life gets hard. The bills don't stop when your heart is broken. The needs don't disappear when you're battling sickness, depression, betrayal, or burnout. Sometimes, the most devoted mothers are also the most depleted ones who are parenting through private pain while praying their children never notice.

You may be holding it all together on the outside, but God sees the weight on your soul. You don't have to pretend with Him. He is not asking you to be superhuman. He's asking you to be surrendered.

Parenting with pain doesn't disqualify you from being a godly mother. In fact, it may shape your prayers with greater depth, compassion, and power. When you're parenting through trauma, grief, chronic illness, mental health struggles, or loneliness, remember that your tears are anointed, your weariness is seen, and your faith, even if faint, is fierce. This level of faith is still enough to move mountains.

Biblical Example: *Hagar in the Wilderness (Genesis 21:14–19)*

Hagar was a single mother sent away into the desert with her son. When her water ran out and her hope dried up, she wept. God heard her cries and sent an angel to remind her that He would make a great nation through her son. Then, God opened her eyes to see a well.

Sometimes, all we need is for God to open our eyes to the well of grace right in front of us.

Confessions & Declarations
Speak these truths found in God's Word regardless of how you may feel:

"God sees my pain, my struggle, and hears my silent prayers."

"I don't have to have it all together. God is my strength when I am weak."

"Even in pain, I am still chosen, still called, and still capable through Christ."

"My children are being shaped by my dependence on God."

"I declare that healing, help, and strength are coming to my household."

"God is redeeming every hard moment and using it for His glory."

"I will not parent from fear, but from faith, even if circumstances look the contrary."

"My children will rise up and call me blessed. Not because I was perfect, but because I stayed faithful."

Prayer

Father, You know the pain I carry...the wounds I rarely voice, and the weariness I try to hide. I lay my burdens at Your feet. Thank You for loving me in the mess. Thank You for parenting me while I parent them. Give me grace for every moment, strength for every task, and hope for every tomorrow. Remind me that even this pain has purpose. Use my story as a testimony of Your sustaining power. In Jesus' name, Amen.

Journal Prompt

What pain am I carrying that I haven't invited God into yet?

How has God sustained me through hard seasons before, and how do I want and need Him to show up now?

Confessions of A Godly Mother

Chapter 10

When You're Co-Parenting or Single

Praying with Strength, Confidence, and
Peace in the Absence of Support

"For your Maker is your husband, The Lord of hosts is His name... For the Lord has called you like a woman forsaken and grieved in spirit..." – Isaiah 54:5–6 (NKJV)

Reflection

You never imagined parenting alone. Maybe it happened through divorce, death, or desertion. Maybe you never married. Or perhaps you're in a co-parenting relationship that feels more like a battlefield than a bridge.

No matter the circumstances, the truth remains that you are not a half-mother. You are not broken, incomplete, or failing simply because you're parenting without another adult at your side. God doesn't reduce your influence, impact, or the power of your prayers because of your relationship status.

He sees your sacrifice. He strengthens your arms. He becomes your ever-present help, your covering, your provider, and your peace.

Whether you're managing schedules, wiping tears, praying through bitterness, or simply trying to survive another day without collapsing, God is holding you. He sees and honors the unseen.

You don't parent alone. Not when Holy Spirit is within you, surrounding your home, and reaching into every room of your child's life. He even enters the places you can't.

Biblical Example: *The Widow of Zarephath (1 Kings 17:8–16)*

This single mother was gathering sticks to prepare her final meal when God sent the prophet Elijah to her doorstep, making a seemingly interesting request at such a dire time—a famine. Elijah asked, *"Please bring me a little water in a cup, that I may drink...Please bring me a morsel of bread in your hand."* She obeyed in faith and what little she had never ran out.

God doesn't ignore the limited places in your life. He performs miracles in them. If He sustained her household through famine, He can sustain yours through every emotional, financial, and spiritual need you have.

Confessions & Declarations
Speak these truths knowing you are never alone:

> "God is the head of my home, the strength in my soul, and the source of everything I need."

> "My child is not lacking love or covering because God fills every gap."

> "I will not compare my family story. I trust God to redeem it with beauty and power."

> "I choose forgiveness, faith, and peace; even when the other parent fails or isn't present."

> "I declare that I am not parenting alone. I am led, empowered, and covered by God."

> "My home is filled with peace, not chaos; love, not bitterness."

> "My child is secure, supported, and surrounded by divine favor."

"God is multiplying my strength and restoring every place of lack."

Prayer

Father, I give You my home, my heart, and my motherhood. You know the weight I carry. You see the moments I cry after the kids are asleep. Show me how to parent with grace, even when I'm stretched thin. Heal every place where co-parenting has become conflict. Replenish every gap with Your presence. Cover my child. Strengthen my spirit with Your amazing grace. Multiply what I offer. Let our home be a refuge built on Your faithfulness. In Jesus' name, Amen.

Journal Prompt

Where do I feel most overwhelmed in this parenting season?

What does God want me to know about His role as my covering and my co-parent?

Cassandra V. Fulwood

Chapter 11

When You're a Spiritual Mother

Praying with Authority and Compassion Over Children You Didn't Birth But Are Called to Cover

"Village life ceased, it ceased in Israel, until I, Deborah, arose, arose a mother in Israel."
– Judges 5:7 (NKJV)

Reflection

You may not have given birth to them. You may not share their DNA. But in the Kingdom of God, motherhood is not just biological. It is spiritual.

Spiritual mothers are mentors, intercessors, role models, and nurturers. They may be aunties, godmothers, stepmothers, foster mothers, grandmothers, pastors, teachers, or faithful women who said "yes" to standing in the gap for someone else's child.

Maybe you're raising children you didn't birth. Maybe you're loving children someone else walked away from. Maybe you've never had your own children, but your arms are still full because your calling is full.

Live in the truth that God doesn't only honor wombs. He honors assignments. If God placed a child on your heart, in your care, or within your influence, you have divine authority to pray over their lives.

Your prayers are just as powerful. Your words carry just as much weight. Your love, your time, and your teaching are invaluable. It's Kingdom motherhood.

Biblical Example: *Mordecai to Esther* (Esther 2:7–17) *and Naomi to Ruth (Ruth 3 & 4)*

Though not her biological father, Mordecai raised Esther as his own and gave her wisdom that would shape her future and deliver a nation. His spiritual covering helped her discover her destiny.

In a similar fashion, although Boaz had taken notice of Ruth, her union with him was sealed under the auspices of Naomi, resulting in protection and provision for both women.

Like Mordecai and Naomi, your presence and prayers may be the very thing that propels a child into their purpose…into places of provision and protection.

Confessions & Declarations
Speak these truths in confidence of who you know God has created you to be in the lives of so many others:

"I am a mother in the Spirit. I am called, chosen, and equipped."

"I may not have given birth, but I am birthing purpose, faith, and identity in this child."

"God has entrusted me with this influence, and I will steward it well."

"I will not compare my journey. I will walk confidently in my assignment."

"I declare that the children I cover will walk in purpose and fulfillment."

"They are protected, loved, and anchored in God's truth."

"I speak life into their destiny, healing into their wounds, and wisdom into their decisions."

"The Spirit of the Lord is upon me to mother, mentor, and lead with compassion and power."

Cassandra V. Fulwood

Prayer

God, thank You for the gift of spiritual motherhood. Thank You for every child You've placed under my influence, whether in my home, my church, my classroom, my place of employment, or my heart. Teach me how to guide them with wisdom. Show me how to love them with purity. Let my prayers shape their identity and destiny. Remind me that I don't have to give birth to be used by You. I carry Your nurture, Your truth, and Your anointing. May my spiritual motherhood change lives and reflect Your glory. In Jesus' name, Amen.

Journal Prompt

Who has God called me to cover and mother in this season?

What has God shown me about the power of spiritual motherhood?

Confessions of A Godly Mother

Chapter 12

When They're Struggling with Mental Health

Praying Clarity, Healing, and Wholeness
Over Emotional and Mental Battles

*"God has not given us a spirit of fear,
but of power and of love and of a sound mind."*
– 2 Timothy 1:7 (NKJV)

Reflection

There is a unique kind of ache when you see your child battling in their mind. When they're anxious, withdrawn, angry, depressed, or overwhelmed, and you feel powerless to fix it. Whether they're too young to articulate it or old enough to hide it behind a mask, you sense it in your spirit. Something is off. They're hurting.

You may be wondering: "Did I miss something?" "Is this my fault?" "Am I enough to help them?" Here's the real deal: You may not have caused it, but through Christ, you can cover it.

Mental health challenges don't disqualify your child from God's purpose. They don't disqualify you from being an effective, godly mother. In fact, this may be the exact battle that shapes your prayer life into something fierce and fiery.

When medicine isn't enough and words fall short, your intercession reaches where no therapist or diagnosis can go...into the deep, hidden places of the soul. You are not powerless. You are a warrior. Even if your child doesn't know it, your prayers are doing the lifting.

Biblical Example: *The Demon-Tormented Boy (Mark 9:14–29)*

A desperate father brought his son to Jesus after watching him suffer for years. The disciples couldn't help, but Jesus could. He rebuked the torment and told the father, *"If you can believe, all things are possible to him who believes.."*

The father cried out, *"Lord, I believe; help my unbelief!"*

That's the prayer of many mothers in this season: "Lord, I believe You can heal my child. But help the part of me that is afraid, exhausted, or unsure." Jesus still meets us right there with compassion and strength.

Confessions & Declarations
Speak and confess these truths over your child and their mental health:

> "God is not afraid of my child's struggle, and neither am I."
>
> "I will not parent in fear, but in faith, even when I don't understand what they're feeling."
>
> "I will not carry shame or blame. God has entrusted me to love, pray, and walk with them through this."
>
> "My child is not broken. They are deeply loved and never beyond the reach of God's healing."
>
> "I declare that my child has a sound mind, a stable heart, and a future filled with peace."
>
> "Every lie, torment, or trauma is being broken by the power of Jesus' name."
>
> "My child will live and not die. They will rise up with strength and clarity."

"Their identity is in Christ; not in a diagnosis, a dark thought, or a bad day."

Prayer

Father, You are the God who speaks peace to storms. Speak now, as only You can, to the storm in my child's mind. Where there is confusion, bring clarity. Where there is torment, bring calm. Where there is depression, bring light. Where there is anxiety, bring confidence. I surrender my fear and stand in the gap with faith. Let healing begin, whether through Your Word, wise counsel, and/or a miracle. Help me walk beside them with patience, love, and discernment. I believe You can heal. I believe You will heal. In Jesus' name, Amen.

Journal Prompt

What do I believe God is showing me about my child's mental health journey?

Where do I need His strength to stand firm and continue interceding?

Cassandra V. Fulwood

Chapter 13

When You're Battling Shame as a Mother

Praying Through Guilt, Regret, and the Grace to Begin Again

"They looked to Him and were radiant, and their faces were not ashamed."
– Psalm 34:5 (NKJV)

Reflection

Shame doesn't always shout. Sometimes, it whispers. "You messed up again." "You should've done more." "Your past disqualifies you from being a good mother." "Your child wouldn't be this way if you were better."

Sound familiar? Shame is the silent weight that many mothers carry...sometimes for years. It attaches itself to your missteps, your wounds, your mistakes, and your weaknesses. Its mission is clear. Its purpose is to make you feel unworthy of the title "godly mother."

But God's truth is laced with so much grace. There is no condemnation for those who are in Christ Jesus. (Romans 8:1) You are not raising your children because you're perfect. You're raising them because God called you, covered you, and is continuing to change you.

You may have lost your temper. You may have missed seasons. You may be walking through tough times. But shame is not your portion. God's amazing grace is.

Every day is a new opportunity to confess truth, speak life, and begin again.

Biblical Example: *The Woman Caught in Adultery (John 8:1–11)*

They brought her to Jesus in shame, expecting judgment. Instead, Jesus knelt, wrote in the dirt, and stood up with grace. He said, *"Neither do I condemn you; go and sin no more."*

Jesus didn't ignore her past. He rewrote her future. He'll do the same for every mother who brings her shame to Him.

Confessions & Declarations

Confess and embrace these truths:

> "I am not a perfect mother, but I am a forgiven one."

> "God sees my heart, not just my history."

> "I will no longer parent from a place of guilt, but from a place of grace."

> "Shame is not my story. Redemption is."

> "I declare that I am a godly mother. Not because of my record, but because of Jesus' righteousness."

> "My past does not disqualify me because God has already redeemed it."

> "I walk in confidence, forgiveness, and new beginnings."

> "My children will see a woman who rises, not one who hides."

Prayer

Jesus, I bring You the hidden places of shame in my heart. The regrets. The "should-haves." The mistakes I replay in my mind. I give them all to You. Wash me. Heal me. Free me. I don't want to parent through guilt.

I want to parent through grace. You don't expect perfection, but You do require surrender. Let my story be one of redemption and freedom for my children to see and follow. In Your name, Amen.

Journal Prompt

What lies has shame whispered to me as a mother?

What truth from God's Word can I begin confessing instead?

Confessions of A Godly Mother

Chapter 14

When You're Praying for Generations to Come

Praying Legacy, Inheritance, and Revival Over Your Bloodline

"But the mercy of the Lord is from everlasting to everlasting on those who fear Him, and His righteousness to children's children."
– Psalm 103:17 (NKJV)

Reflection

Some of your most powerful prayers will be for people you'll never meet, including grandchildren, great-grandchildren, and descendants yet unborn.

Your motherhood is not just for the moment. It's for the movement. The movement of generations.

When you pray, you're not just covering tantrums, test scores, and teen drama. You're digging wells. You're planting oaks. You're sowing into spiritual legacies that will carry the presence of God for generations.

You may not have come from a godly bloodline. But through Christ, you're building one. You are the turning point. You are the one who breaks the cycle. You are the one who starts the new thing. You are the one whose prayers will echo into your family tree long after you're gone. Your ceiling will become their floor. They will stand on your shoulders because you knelt on your knees. Your intercession will become their inheritance.

Biblical Example: *Lois and Eunice (2 Timothy 1:5)*

Paul praised Timothy's sincere faith and traced it back through the two generations of his mother, Eunice, and his grandmother, Lois. These women weren't preachers on platforms. They were faithful women who poured Scripture and prayer into a boy who would change the world.

You may never hold a microphone, but if you hold your family up in prayer, you're shaping world changers.

Confessions & Declarations

Declare these truths over the next generations:

"My prayers are building a foundation for the generations that follow me."

"I am a matriarch of faith and righteousness in my family line."

"The cycles of sin, addiction, fear, and shame end with me."

"I will pass down more than traditions. I will pass down truth. God's truth that makes one free."

"I declare that my children, grandchildren, great-grandchildren, and those down to a thousand generations will walk in the fear of the Lord."

"They will fulfill divine assignments, live holy lives, and love Jesus with all their hearts."

"Revival will run through my bloodline. Every generation will know the Lord."

"I will leave a spiritual inheritance of faith, fire, and fruitfulness."

Prayer

God of Abraham, Isaac, and Jacob, be the God of my lineage. Let my ceiling be the floor for my descendants.

I lift up every child who will come from me, through me, or around me. I declare salvation, blessing, favor, and purpose over them. Let not one fall away. Let every generation grow stronger in faith, deeper in truth, and more on fire for You. Even when I am gone, let my prayers remain active. Let my legacy be one of godliness. In Jesus' name, Amen.

Journal Prompt

What do I want to leave behind spiritually for the generations after me?

What promises or Scriptures do I feel led to pray into my family line?

Cassandra V. Fulwood

Chapter 15

When You Feel Spiritually Empty

Praying From a Dry Place
and Receiving the Strength to Revive

*"He gives power to the weak, and to those who have
no might He increases strength."*
– Isaiah 40:29 (NKJV)

Reflection

You love God. You believe in prayer. You've spoken life over your children. But deep down, you feel dry.

You're showing up for everyone else, but your own soul is parched. You're whispering, "God, help" more than "God, thank You." You're nodding through the devotionals, but your heart is distant. You feel guilty for even admitting it, but you're spiritually tired.

You are not a bad mother for being empty. You are a human mother who's poured out more than she's received. Even Jesus withdrew from the crowds to be replenished (Luke 5:16). So can you.

There's no shame in needing rest, revival, or refreshment. There is only grace. Return to the feet of Jesus, to the well that never runs dry, to the One who restores the soul of every weary woman.

The most godly thing you can do in your emptiness is not hide it, but bring it to the Healer.

Biblical Example: *The Woman at the Well (John 4:4–26)*

She came with an empty jar and a broken past. She expected to draw water. Instead, she encountered the Living Water. In one conversation with Jesus, she was seen, known, forgiven, and filled. She left her water jar behind because He satisfied her with something more fulfilling.

You don't have to keep drawing from dry places. Come to the Well.

Confessions & Declarations
Confess and declare that you will rise again:

"God, I admit I'm tired. I've poured out more than I've received. Fill me."

"I'm not ashamed of my need. I bring it to You."

"You are not disappointed in me. You are drawing me back to Yourself."

"I choose rest. I choose grace. I choose to be filled again."

"I declare that my soul is being refreshed even now."

"The Lord is restoring my joy, passion, and strength."

"I will not parent from pressure but from presence."

"I am not running on empty. I am drinking deeply from the Well that never runs dry."

Prayer

Jesus, I need You. Not just as Savior, but as my Restorer. I'm tired. I feel disconnected. I'm going through the motions, but my spirit is dry. I don't want to parent from a place of spiritual burnout. So, I come back to You. Fill me again. Speak to me again. Restore the joy of my salvation. Rekindle the fire in my prayers and passion in my worship. Let me mother from the overflow of Your presence, not the leftovers of my energy. In Your name, Amen.

Journal Prompt

What's been draining me spiritually in this season?

What small steps can I take today to reconnect with the heart of God?

Confessions of A Godly Mother

Chapter 16

When They're Called Into Ministry

Praying Courage, Humility, and Endurance
Over a Child Chosen to Lead

"Before I formed you in the womb I knew you; Before you were born I sanctified you; I ordained you a prophet to the nations." – Jeremiah 1:5 (NKJV)

Reflection

When you sense that your child is called into ministry, whether as a preacher, worship leader, teacher, evangelist, missionary, or servant leader, it's holy, humbling, and heavy. There's joy and pride, yes. But also a weight. A sense that this road will not be easy.

You know the price of ministry. You know the pain that can come with serving people. You've seen leaders praised one moment and persecuted the next. And now, God is calling your child into that world?

That's why this season demands a different kind of motherhood. You are not just praying for protection. You're praying for spiritual endurance, humility, and intimacy with Jesus.

It's tempting to want to shelter them from the weight of the call. Instead, God is asking you to cover them in the Spirit and release them in faith.

You're not just raising a leader. You're raising someone who may help lead a generation into revival. Your prayers are equipping them for battle.

Biblical Example: *Mary, Mother of Jesus*

Mary wasn't just raising a son. She was raising the Savior. She saw Him perform miracles, and she saw Him suffer. She stood at the foot of the cross and watched His calling cost Him everything. Even before that, she was faithful to steward His purpose from a young age. She pondered it. Protected it. Prayed through it.

Like Mary, you may not understand everything about your child's calling, but you can protect it with prayer.

Confessions & Declarations

Pray this prayer and confessions for children called into any aspect of ministry:

"God has called my child, and I release them into His purpose, not mine."

"I will not fear the cost of their calling. I will trust the One who called them."

"I will not compare their ministry to someone else's. I will celebrate their unique assignment."

"I may not be on the platform, but I will always be on my knees."

"I declare that my child walks in humility, purity, and bold obedience."

"Their ministry will be rooted in intimacy, not performance."

"They will preach truth, carry grace, and reflect Jesus in all they do."

"They are anointed, appointed, and protected for such a time as this."

Prayer

Lord, thank You for calling my child. Whether they speak to many or serve in secret, I bless the mantle You've placed on their life. Give them wisdom beyond their years, strength to endure trials, and grace to walk humbly. Let them never be impressed by the spotlight but forever drawn to Your presence. Use me to encourage them, not control them. Cover them from pride, burnout, or compromise. Help me steward their calling with intercession, patience, and joy. In Jesus' name, Amen.

Journal Prompt

What fears or expectations do I need to release about my child's calling?

How can I intentionally support their spiritual growth, character development, and calling in general?

Cassandra V. Fulwood

Chapter 17

When You're Praying Through Crisis

Calling on God in Moments of Chaos,
Fear, and Emergency

"God is our refuge and strength, a very present help in trouble." – Psalm 46:1 (KJV)

Reflection

There are moments in motherhood that bring you to your knees without warning. A phone call, a diagnosis, a late-night emergency, a sudden loss, a terrifying situation. In these moments, all the usual words disappear, and all you can say is: *"Jesus, help."*

And He does.

Crisis is the place where panic meets presence. It's where God doesn't wait for eloquent prayers; He answers the cries of a desperate mother. The tears, the groans, the silent pleas are all heard in heaven.

You may not have time for a quiet time, a scripture journal, or a worship playlist when (not if) crisis hits. But if you can say His name, if you can whisper *"God, I trust You,"* even when trembling, you are standing in authority.

A godly mother in crisis is not helpless. She is hidden under the shadow of the Almighty (Psalm 91). She prays from a place of covering and covenant, even when everything around her is shaking.

Biblical Example: *The Shunammite Woman (2 Kings 4:8–37)*

When her son suddenly died in her arms, the Shunammite woman didn't panic. She didn't collapse. She placed the child on the prophet's bed and said three powerful words: *"It is well."* Even in crisis, she spoke faith.

God honored her courage, and through Elisha, her son was brought back to life.

Even in crisis, your faith has resurrection power.

Confessions & Declarations

Speak these truths when in a crisis:

> "God is with me in the storm, and I will not be moved."

> "Even when I don't understand, I will not stop trusting."

> "God hears me the first time. He sees me. He is already working."

> "This crisis did not catch God off guard, and He will bring me through it."

> "I declare peace over my mind, stability in my home, and divine intervention in this situation."

> "God is fighting for me and my child. We will not be shaken."

> "Angels are encamped around us, and we are protected on every side."

> "What the enemy meant for evil, God is already turning for good."

Prayer

Lord, I feel overwhelmed, but I refuse to be overcome. I invite You into this crisis. Bring peace where there is panic. Speak truth where there are lies. I plead the blood of Jesus over my child, my household, and this situation. Silence every voice of fear. I choose to believe that You are working, even when I can't see it. Thank You for being the God who rescues, restores, and redeems. In Jesus' mighty name, Amen.

Journal Prompt

What is one area of this crisis I need to surrender completely to God?

What has God done for me in the past that reminds me He will be faithful again?

Confessions of A Godly Mother

Cassandra V. Fulwood

Part 3:

The PowerSpeak Toolkit

Declarations About Your Children

These declarations are bold, Spirit-led truths spoken in alignment with God's Word. When you declare over your children, you are not just stating what is; you are calling forth what God has promised. These are not wishful thoughts. They are faith-filled proclamations that shift atmospheres, renew identity, and shape destiny. Whether your child is near or far, walking with the Lord or wandering, your declarations carry weight. A mother's voice, aligned with heaven, is one of the most powerful forces on earth.

Identity & Purpose

"I will praise You, for I am fearfully and wonderfully made; marvelous are Your works, and that my soul knows very well." – Psalm 139:14 (NKJV)

- I declare that my child knows who they are and Whose they are.
- They find their identity in the Name, Image, and Likeness of their Creator.
- They are chosen, accepted, and set apart for divine purpose.

- They are not defined by mistakes, labels, or opinions, but by the Word of God.
- They will fulfill the purpose for which they were born.

Salvation & Faith

"...Believe on the Lord Jesus Christ, and you will be saved, you and your household." – Acts 16:31 (NKJV)

- I declare that my child belongs to Jesus and walks in faith.
- They will love the Lord with all their heart, soul, mind, and strength.
- They are rooted in the Word and led by Holy Spirit.
- They will not turn away from truth but will grow in grace and godliness.

Protection & Safety

"The Lord shall preserve you from all evil; He shall preserve your soul." – Psalm 121:7 (NKJV)

- I declare that my child is protected from harm, danger, and evil.

- Angels are assigned to guard them day and night.
- No weapon formed against them shall prosper.
- They walk in divine covering and safety wherever they go.

Wisdom & Decision-Making

"If any of you lacks wisdom, let him ask of ask God... and it will be given to him." – James 1:5 (NKJV)

- I declare that my child walks in wisdom beyond their years.
- They make sound, godly decisions in every season.
- They are quick to hear God's voice and obey. They refuse to follow the crowd.
- Holy Spirit leads them in all truth.

Friendships & Relationships

"He who walks with wise men will be wise, but the companion of fools will be destroyed." – Proverbs 13:20 (NKJV)

- I declare that my child is surrounded by godly friends and mentors.
- They are not influenced by toxic people but are influencers for Christ.
- They choose relationships that align with their values and purpose.
- Their heart is protected and their boundaries are honored.

Emotional & Mental Health

"You will keep him in perfect peace, whose mind is stayed on You, because he trusts in You." – Isaiah 26:3 (NKJV)

- I declare that my child has the mind of Christ and the peace of God.
- Anxiety, fear, depression, and confusion must leave.
- Their thoughts are healthy, whole, and aligned with truth.
- They have soundness of mind, joy in their soul, and strength in their emotions.

Academic & Career Success

"Commit your works to the Lord, and your thoughts will be established." – Proverbs 16:3 (NKJV)

- I declare that my child is focused, diligent, and successful in their studies and/or work.
- They excel in learning, grow in creativity, and operate in excellence.
- Doors of opportunity open for them, and they walk through them with confidence.
- Everything they put their hands to will prosper.

Health & Healing

"...and with his stripes we are healed." – Isaiah 53:5 (KJV)

- I declare that my child walks in divine health and healing.
- Every sickness, disease, and disorder must bow to the name of Jesus.
- Their body is strong, their immune system is fortified, and their energy is renewed.
- Healing flows through every cell, system, and organ in their body.

Purity & Holiness

"How can a young man cleanse his way? By taking heed according to Your word." – Psalm 119:9 (NKJV)

- I declare that my child honors God with their body, mind, and heart.
- They are set apart, not swayed by culture, and walk in sexual purity.
- They resist temptation and cling to righteousness.
- Holiness is their desire, and the Word of God is their standard.

Calling & Ministry

"For the gifts and the calling of God are irrevocable." – Romans 11:29 (NKJV)

- I declare that my child hears and obeys the call of God on their life.
- They serve with humility, lead with integrity, and speak with boldness.
- Their gifts are stirred, their purpose is unfolding, and their impact is eternal.
- They will fulfill every assignment God has written for them.

Blessings to Confess Over Children

These confessions of blessings are designed to be spoken regularly at bedtime, before school, after discipline, or any quiet moment when your words can shape their spirit. They are rooted in Scripture and filled with prophetic encouragement. Whether your child is a baby or an adult, your confessions and blessings hold power.

Morning Blessing Before School or Starting the Day

"This is the day the Lord has made; we will rejoice and be glad in it.." – Psalm 118:24 (NKJV)

- I bless you with joy, focus, and peace today.
- May your heart be full of courage and your mind be clear and sharp.
- May you walk in kindness and truth and make wise choices.
- You are protected, loved, and never alone.
- The angels of the Lord are encamped about you to keep you in all your ways.
- The Lord is with you in every classroom, hallway, and conversation.

Bedtime Blessing for Rest and Peace

"I will both lie down in peace, and sleep; for You alone, O Lord, make me dwell in safety." – Psalm 4:8 (NKJV)

- I bless your body with sweet rest and your dreams with peace.
- May angels surround you and the presence of God settle over you like a warm, weighted blanket.
- May your heart be still, your mind be quiet, and your spirit be refreshed.
- You are safe, loved, and in God's care tonight and always.

Blessing Over Your Entire Family Line

"...I will pour out My Spirit on your descendants, and My blessing on your offspring." – Isaiah 44:3 (NKJV)

- I bless this bloodline with revival, righteousness, and restoration.
- May every generation love and serve the Lord wholeheartedly.
- May strongholds be destroyed, cycles stopped, and legacy established in Christ.

- My family is covered by the blood of Jesus, filled with the Spirit, and walking in divine purpose.

Prayers for the Mother's Soul

These prayers are written for the weary days, the hidden moments, the battles no one sees, and the seasons when you need to be reminded that God is mothering you while you mother others.

A Prayer for Strength

"...for the joy of the Lord is your strength." – Nehemiah 8:10 (NKJV)

Lord, today I need Your supernatural strength. I'm tired mentally, emotionally, spiritually. I don't want to mother in my own might. Fill me with Your joy and refresh me with Your presence. Let me laugh again, hope again, and walk in the strength that only You provide. In Jesus' name, Amen.

A Prayer for Wisdom

"If any of you lacks wisdom, let him ask of God...and it will be given to him." – James 1:5 (NKJV)

Father, You know the situations in front of me. You see the questions I don't have answers to. I ask for wisdom. Not just knowledge but holy insight. Show me how to lead, when to speak, when to hold back, and how to parent in alignment with You. Thank You for being my Counselor and my Guide. In Jesus' name, Amen.

A Prayer for Peace in Chaos

"You will keep in perfect peace whose mind is stayed on You, because he trusts in You." – Isaiah 26:3 (NKJV)

Lord, the noise of motherhood is loud. There are so many needs, emotions, and tasks. You are my stillness. Quiet my racing thoughts and anxious heart. Help me stay rooted in Your peace no matter what the day brings. Speak peace over my mind, and let me bring peace into my home. In Jesus' name, Amen.

A Prayer for Forgiveness and New Beginnings

"They are new every morning: great is thy faithfulness."
– Lamentations 3:23 (KJV)

God, I confess the moments I've fallen short by losing my temper, rushing past my children, and forgetting to pray. Thank You that Your mercy meets me every single morning. I receive Your forgiveness and walk in fresh grace today. Help me extend that same grace to myself and my children. In Jesus' name, Amen.

A Prayer for Emotional Healing

"He heals the brokenhearted and binds up their wounds." – Psalm 147:3 (NKJV)

Father, I bring You every wound I've tried to ignore…disappointment, betrayal, unspoken grief. Heal what's been hiding in me. Restore the broken places. Help me not to parent from pain but from wholeness. I receive Your love in the places where I've felt unseen. In Jesus' name, Amen.

A Prayer for Confidence

"Strength and honour are her clothing; and she shall rejoice in time to come." – Proverbs 31:25 (KJV)

Lord, some days I doubt myself. Am I doing enough? Am I getting it right? But, today, I choose to put on confidence; not in my ability, but in Your calling. You chose me for this child. You equipped me for this assignment. I am clothed in Your strength, and I will walk boldly. In Jesus' name, Amen.

A Prayer for God's Presence in My Parenting

"Except the Lord build the house, they labour in vain that build it…" – Psalm 127:1 (KJV)

Holy Spirit, be in my home. Be in my voice, my reactions, my guidance, and my boundaries. I don't want to parent from culture or emotion. I want to parent from Your presence. Build this house with Your wisdom and fill it with Your peace. In Jesus' name, Amen.

Scriptures to Meditate Upon Regarding Your Children

God's Word is the anchor in every season of motherhood. These scriptures have been handpicked to speak directly to the heart of a mother, whether you're interceding for your child's protection, salvation, identity, healing, or future. Meditate on them slowly. Write them in your journal. Speak them over your children. Pray them back to God. His Word never returns void. As you let it take root in your spirit, it will grow into confidence, peace, and faith that lasts through every storm.

Mental & Emotional Health

- Overcoming Anxiety & Fear (*Philippians 4:6-7; 2 Timothy 1:7*)

- Breaking Free from Depression & Hopelessness (*Psalm 34:17-18; Isaiah 41:10*)

- Healing from Suicidal Thoughts, Ideations, and Tendencies (*Psalm 42:11; Jeremiah 29:11; John 10:10*)

- Developing a Sound & Peaceful Mind (*Isaiah 26:3; Romans 12:2*)

- Building Self-Esteem & Godly Confidence (*Psalm 139:14; Ephesians 2:10; Philippians 1:6*)
- Breaking Free from Eating Disorders & Unhealthy Body Image (*1 Corinthians 6:19-20; 1 Samuel 16:7*)
- Healing from Past Trauma & Emotional Wounds (*Psalm 147:3; 2 Corinthians 1:3-4*)

Spiritual Growth & Faith Development

- Trusting God in All Things (*Proverbs 3:5-6; Hebrews 11:6*)
- Seeking God with a Whole Heart (*Matthew 6:33; Jeremiah 29:13*)
- Committing Their Life to God (*Romans 10:9 & 10; 12:1; Joshua 24:15*)
- Developing a Strong Prayer Life (*Luke 18:1; 1 Thessalonians 5:16-18; James 5:16*)
- Walking in the Power of Holy Spirit (*Acts 1:8; Romans 8:14; Galatians 5:22-23*)
- Receiving and Using Spiritual Gifts (*1 Corinthians 12:4-7; 2 Timothy 1:6-7*)
- Breaking Free from Generational Curses & Strongholds (*Galatians 3:13; 2 Corinthians 10:4*)

Relationships & Marriage (Present & Future)

- Choosing Godly Friends & Relationships (*Proverbs 13:20; 1 Corinthians 15:33*)
- Protection from Toxic Relationships & Abusive Influences (*Psalm 1:1-3; Proverbs 4:23*)
- Preparing for a Future Godly Spouse (*Proverbs 18:22; 2 Corinthians 6:14*)
- Praying for Their Current or Future Marriage (*Ephesians 5:22-25; Colossians 3:14-15*)
- Walking in Purity & Sexual Integrity (*1 Corinthians 6:18-20; 1 Thessalonians 4:3-4*)

Finances, Career, & Purpose

- Godly Wisdom in Finances & Stewardship (*Proverbs 21:5, 20; 22:7; Psalm 37:21*)
- Breaking Free from Poverty Mindsets & Lack (*Deuteronomy 8:18; Psalm 23:1; Philippians 4:19*)
- Walking in Prosperity & Divine Favor (*Psalm 1:3; 35:27; 3 John 1:2*)
- Success & Excellence in Career, Work, & Business (*Colossians 3:23-24; Proverbs 18:16*)
- Discovering & Walking in Their God-Given Purpose (*Proverbs 19:21; Ephesians 2:10; 5:15-17*)

Cassandra V. Fulwood

Protection, Deliverance, & Warfare

- Divine Protection from Harm, Accidents, & Attacks (*Psalm 91:1-4; Isaiah 54:17*)

- Deliverance from Addictions & Bondages (*Matthew 11:28-30; John 8:36; 2 Corinthians 3:17*)

- Overcoming the Spirit of Rebellion & Disobedience (*Ephesians 6:1-3; Proverbs 22:6*)

- Breaking the Power of Peer Pressure & Worldly Influences (*Romans 12:2; 1 John 2:15-17*)

- Victory Over the Enemy in Spiritual Warfare (*Ephesians 6:10-18; 2 Corinthians 10:3-5*)

Character & Integrity Development

- Cultivating a Spirit of Humility & Servanthood (*Philippians 2:3-9; Matthew 23:11-12*)

- Walking in Truth & Integrity (*Proverbs 11:3; Psalm 15:1-2*)

- Developing a Heart of Gratitude & Contentment (*1 Thessalonians 5:18; Philippians 4:11-12*)

- Cultivating a Lifestyle of Generosity & Giving (*2 Corinthians 9:6-7; Acts 20:35*)

Afterword

There comes a moment after the declarations have been made, the confessions whispered through tears, and the Scriptures spoken into the stillness when you realize that you weren't just reading a book. You were being rebuilt. Page by page, prayer by prayer, something in you has shifted. This wasn't information. It was impartation. It was Holy Spirit breathing fresh strength into dry places and placing prophetic oil into your hands because a mother who knows who she is in God cannot be silenced.

You weren't just learning how to mother better. You were awakening to your calling. You weren't just encouraged. You were commissioned. Standing at the end of these pages, you must ask yourself, "What now?" Simply and wholeheartedly, you must walk in it.

Walk in the truths you've declared. Stand on the Scriptures you've meditated on. Embrace the authority you've been given. Not as a perfect woman, but as a yielded one. Yielded mothers shift generations. They war in secret, and heaven honors them in public.

You may have started this book feeling unseen, maybe even broken. But God never needed you to be whole to use you. He needed you to be willing. You were willing, and that's where legacy begins.

Legacy isn't about perfection. It's not about being the loudest, the most organized, or even the most spiritual. Legacy is about obedience in motion. It's about saying yes when your flesh screams no. It's about whispering prayers when your heart is weary. It's about prophesying over your children when they look nothing like what God promised you. You may not see the harvest right away, but make no mistake…your hands are planting seeds in eternal soil.

Every spiritual mother in Scripture knew how to war before she ever saw breakthrough. Sarah had to believe beyond barrenness. Hannah had to pray through deep anguish. Ruth had to leave behind her past and cleave to a new people, trusting God to redeem her future. Naomi had to guide in grief. Deborah had to rise in national crisis. Jochebed had to release her baby into a river, trusting that God's hand would guide Moses to safety. The Canaanite woman had to press past rejection and fight for her daughter's healing with relentless faith. Elizabeth had to carry promise in her old age, becoming the mother of the forerunner to the Messiah. Mary had to release her son to fulfill a destiny that would pierce her own soul. These women were warriors, intercessors, nurturers, and visionaries. Like you, they learned that breakthrough rarely comes without a battle.

You are in a divine lineage of women who said yes in silence and shook nations without applause. Women who wept behind closed doors and birthed movements in secret.

So, as you close this book, don't close your heart. Don't close your prayer life. Don't close your mouth. Open your eyes to what God is doing. Open your spirit to where He is leading. Open your mouth and confess His promises until they become your children's reality.

Speak the Word. Pray with fire. Cry when you must. Rest when you need to. But never, ever quit. Your home is an altar. Your prayers are incense. Your legacy is alive even if it's still growing underground. You don't need to see the full picture to believe in the promise. You don't need to have all the answers to raise a child of destiny. Just keep showing up with your faith and your yes.

You are not raising just sons and daughters. You are raising deliverers, worshipers, prophets, and Kingdom voices. You are covering politicians, teachers, missionaries, entrepreneurs, and revivalists. You are shaping the future, and hell knows it. That's why the battle has been so intense. Lift your head. Square your shoulders. Walk in the fire of your assignment.

You are a watchman. A warrior. A Godly Mother!

With faith, favor, focus, fervent prayer, & fierce love,
Cassandra V. Fulwood

Upcoming Publications

Publication Date: September 2025

It's been ten years in the making!... *5 Miles to Destiny* walks you through the five spiritual miles that often precede your breakthrough: Rejection, Betrayal, Abandonment, Isolation vs. Incubation, & Forgiveness.

Blending personal testimony, biblical wisdom, and the example of bible characters who walked every mile, you will be motivated to know you haven't missed it. You're closer than you think. Keep walking. Destiny is *5 miles* away.

Publication Date: January 2026

In this new edition, you'll find revisions and all-new:

- Breakdown of biblical dreams
- Fresh insights & clarity on visions
- Expanded Symbolism & Imagery

www.ingramcontent.com/pod-product-compliance
Lightning Source LLC
Chambersburg PA
CBHW030447100526
44580CB00002B/23